Envy

Contents

Barbara Mitchelhill

Published in association with
The Basic Skills Agency

Hodder & Stoughton
A MEMBER OF THE HODDER HEADLINE GROUP

Acknowledgements
Cover: Dave Smith
Illustrations: Dave Smith

Orders: please contact Bookpoint Ltd, 78 Milton Park, Abingdon, Oxon OX14
4TD. Telephone: (44) 01235 827720, Fax: (44) 01235 400454. Lines are open
from 9.00–6.00, Monday to Saturday, with a 24 hour message answering service.
Email address: orders@bookpoint.co.uk

British Library Cataloguing in Publication Data
A catalogue record for this title is available from The British Library

ISBN 0 340 80061 5

First published 2001
Impression number   10 9 8 7 6 5 4 3 2 1
Year   2007 2006 2005 2004 2003 2002 2001

Typeset by SX Composing DTP, Rayleigh, Essex.
Printed in Great Britain for Hodder & Stoughton Educational, a division of
Hodder Headline Plc, 338 Euston Road, London NW1 3BH by Athenaeum
Press, Gateshead, Tyne and Wear.

1

The Briefcase

It's funny how small things can change your life.
Look at what happened to Dave Harley last year.
He was sitting on the train in Euston station.
Waiting to go home after a hard day in the office.

Just as the train was about to move off,
a man came into Dave's compartment
and slumped into the seat opposite.
He was out of breath from
running to catch the train.
'Not very fit,' Dave thought.
'He could do with a good workout.'

The man sat back and closed his eyes.
He looked exhausted.
Dave looked at him closely.
'Expensive suit,' he said to himself.
'Expensive briefcase.
Not plastic, like mine. It's leather.'
It was obvious that he was
a businessman – and loaded.
Dave wondered why he wasn't
in First Class.

Suddenly, the man opened his eyes
and made Dave jump.
'Excuse me,' he said leaning forward.
'Would you keep an eye on my briefcase?
I want to get a drink from the buffet.'
Dave nodded.

'Thank you,' the stranger replied as he
struggled to his feet.
Then he walked away down the rocking train.

Once he was gone,
Dave looked closely at the briefcase.
It must have cost a bomb.
He reached out and ran his fingers
over the leather.
It was so soft! So smooth!

He wondered if he would ever be
able to afford a briefcase like that.
Or a designer suit?
They were the kind of things he *really* wanted.
He didn't want to make do
with a plastic briefcase
and suits from the catalogue.
No way! He wanted to be RICH!
He closed his eyes and thought of all the
things he would like.

Half an hour later, he was still dreaming.
A voice over the speaker woke him
with an announcement.
The train was stopping at his station.
He'd be getting off soon.

As he opened his eyes and sat up,
he realised that the seat opposite was still empty.
The man had not returned.
The briefcase was still on the table.

It would be so easy to reach out
and take the case, he thought.
He could get off the train.
By the time the man came back,
it would be too late.
He would be long gone.

The train slowed down as it pulled
into the station.
Dave got to his feet.
His pulse was racing as he looked around
the carriage.
Everyone had their heads in newspapers.
And there was no sign of the man.

As the train lurched to a halt,
Dave grabbed the briefcase.
Then he walked towards the door
and stepped down onto the platform.

2

Stop Thief!

He ran all the way home.
Any minute he expected to hear someone
shout, 'Stop thief!' But nobody did.
By the time he reached the flat
he was gasping for breath.

'Dave!' said Kylie as he stepped into the hall.
'Slow down, love.
You'll give yourself a heart attack.'

Dave leaned against the wall, panting.
'I need a workout,' he said. 'I'm not fit.'
He went into the lounge and slumped onto
the settee.

'I'll make you a cup of tea,' said Kylie.
When she came back, she noticed the briefcase.
'Whose is that?' she asked.

Dave shrugged.
'I won some money on the firm's draw,' he said.
'I thought I'd give myself a treat.'
He was surprised how easily he lied.
He'd never lied to Kylie in the two years
he had known her. How could he?

Kylie picked up the briefcase and looked at it.
'It must have cost a fortune.
How much did you win?'
Dave felt himself panicking. 'Enough,' he said.
'But not enough for me, eh?' Kylie said,
flinging the briefcase on the settee.

Dave grabbed her by the arm.
'Calm down, babe.
I'm taking you out tomorrow night,' he said.
'It was going to be a surprise.
Somewhere special.'
Why had he said that?
He couldn't afford to go somewhere special.

Kylie smiled. 'Fantastic!' she said.
'We haven't been out for weeks.'
And they kissed and made up.

Later, Kylie went and had a bath.
When the bathroom door was shut, Dave
opened the briefcase.
There was nothing important inside, just
some business papers.
One was a bank statement for a
Mr Robert MacKeith.
'Wow!' Dave said as he read it.
'Mr MacKeith is one rich guy.'

He looked in the case again,
checking that it was empty.
There *was* something–
a small roll of paper held with a rubber band.
It was a bundle of fifty pound notes.
There must be five hundred pounds –
maybe more.
Taking Kylie out would be no problem now!
Instead of feeling pleased, Dave felt worried.
He had never stolen anything in his life.

That night he couldn't sleep.
By three o'clock he had decided what to do.
He would keep one fifty pound note.
Enough for the meal he had promised Kylie.
He would put the rest in an envelope
and send it back to Robert MacKeith.

3

Temper!

The next morning Dave read the bank
statement again.
'This guy won't miss a few notes,'
he said to himself.
He took five notes from the roll.
He would buy himself a decent suit
and a new shirt.
The kind he'd always wanted.
That morning he found a fantastic suit.
It was dark blue like his old one.
Kylie would never notice the difference.
This suit was special.
And it made him special, too.

'You look nice,' said Kylie
as they got ready to go out that evening.
'The shirt's lovely.
And I see you've pressed your suit.
You look a real city type, Dave!'
He knew she didn't suspect he had spent so
much money.

'Let's go and have a great night out,' he said.
And they did, too.
They went to a posh restaurant
on the other side of town.
Usually it was too pricey for them.
But that night, they had the works!

When Dave woke up on Sunday,
his head was throbbing.
'Get me a tablet, will you?' he groaned.
'I've got a terrible hangover.'

Kylie smiled as she slipped out of bed.
'OK,' she said.

'Thanks,' said Dave.
And then he remembered his new shirt.
'Do me a favour, babe,' he said.
'Wash and iron that shirt for me, will you?
I want to wear it tomorrow.
I've got an important meeting.'

Kylie raised her eyebrows.
'Have you?' she said.
'You said you were just the dogsbody.'

Dave suddenly felt angry.
'That's all you know!' he snapped.
'Now go and wash my shirt.'

Kylie was shocked.
He was treating her like an unpaid servant.
How dare he!
She stormed out of the bedroom.

Dave slumped against the headboard.
He didn't know why he felt so stroppy.

Why had he lied again?
He didn't have a meeting.
He never had meetings.
He was only the office junior. A nobody.
He opened the newspaper.
A small article at the bottom of the page
caught his eye.

Death on the Rails
The body of millionaire Robert MacKeith,
was found on the line between
Paddington and Reading late
on Friday evening.
It is not clear whether the death
was accidental or whether
he had been pushed.
For some time, the police have had
suspicions about Mr MacKeith.

Dave was stunned. It was the man on the train!
If Robert MacKeith was dead,
he could keep the money!
Relief swept over him.
He didn't feel guilty now.
'Kylie! Kylie!' He called at the top of his voice.

She came bursting through the bedroom door.
'What's wrong?' she said.

Dave held out his arms. 'Nothing, babe!
I wanted to say I'm sorry I was rude to you.'
'OK, just as long as it doesn't happen again,'
she said.

He grinned. 'It won't.
And I've got a surprise for you.
Some shares I bought did really well.
It must be my lucky week.'
He was getting used to lying. It was easy.

'I didn't know you had shares,' Kylie said.
'That's brilliant!'
'So how about a holiday?' said Dave.
'You choose.'

She thought for a minute.
'Let's have a weekend in Devon.'
'Right,' said Dave. 'Devon it is.'
Having money felt good.
But he wondered how long it would last.

4

Envy

The next day Dave put on his new suit.
He felt great.
When he walked into the office,
people looked at him.
Most days he felt invisible.
Today he was the centre of attention.

Later that morning, Harry came over.
'Hey, Dave! You busy?'
Dave didn't like Harry.
But he envied him and his flash car.

Dave replied.
'No, I'm not busy.
Just doing the usual boring things.'
'I was wondering,' Harry said,
'if you were doing anything this weekend.'
Dave shook his head.
'Want to make a bit of dosh?' said Harry.
Dave sat up straight.
He didn't trust Harry but he couldn't
stop himself from asking, 'How do I do that?'

Harry smiled his white, smarmy smile.
'Just pick something up for me in
Amsterdam,' he said.
'I'd do it myself but I'm busy.'
Dave shifted in his seat. He felt uneasy.
Was Harry into smuggling drugs?
'There's £500 in it for you this time.
Maybe more next time.'
Dave's face was covered in amazement.
Harry laughed.
'How do you think I can afford
a sports car on my wage, eh?'

Dave thought all morning about
what Harry had said.
He really wanted to talk to Kylie but
she'd say, 'No.'
She didn't like taking risks.
She wasn't like Dave. He wanted everything.

He soon convinced himself that going to
Amsterdam was no big deal.
He would go. It was easy money.

Later, he met Harry on his way out of the office.
'You thought about Amsterdam?' Harry asked.
'Yeah,' said Dave. 'I'll do the trip.'

Harry grinned.
'I knew you were smart!' he said.
'Come on. We'll go out and celebrate.'
They went to a fancy restaurant.
After that, they went drinking at
The Flamingo Club.
Harry paid for it all.
'It's nothing,' he said at the end of the evening.
'I can afford it!'
Envy suddenly gripped Dave.
He couldn't wait to have more money.
Maybe Amsterdam was the start of the big time.

5

Amsterdam

That weekend Dave set off for Amsterdam.
Harry had given him a suitcase
with a false bottom.
Inside was the cash to pay for the drugs.
Once in Amsterdam,
a taxi took him from the airport to
the old part of the town.
They arrived at the house.
A tall, dark house. Number 127.
Dave went inside clutching the case.

'Don't ask questions,' Harry had said.
'Just give them the money.

They'll hand over the goods and you put them
in the case.'

Everything went exactly to plan.
There were two men in the flat.
It was too dark to see what they looked like.
One of them counted the money.
The other handed over three packets wrapped
in plastic.
Neither of them spoke more than
a couple of words.

When that was done,
Dave headed for the airport and flew home.
But going through Customs was a nightmare.
Everyone seemed to be looking at him.
He did his best to look casual. But it wasn't easy.

'Anything to declare, sir?' a man asked.
Dave's heart pounded so loud
that he thought everyone would hear.
But he flung open his case.
'Only a couple of cans of lager,' he said.
The Customs man smiled.
He rummaged through Dave's clothes.
'Right you are, sir,' he said. 'You can go.'
Dave walked away, shaking with fear.

Harry was pleased the trip had gone well.
'Well done, Dave, my boy!' he said.
'You're a natural!
I can see you're going to be a very rich man.'
And that was how Dave started to live
on the wrong side of the Law.

6

Giving it up

Dave carried on making trips to Europe.
Soon he was going twice, three times a month.
He was earning a lot of money
– but he worried about the risk.
It was only a matter of time
before he was caught.
He felt ill just thinking about it.
'You're working too hard, Dave!' said Kylie.
'You don't look well.

'When can we have that weekend in Devon?.
You know you promised.'

Her nagging was getting on Dave's nerves.
But then everything was getting on his
nerves these days.
What was the point of all this risky business?
He didn't even have time to spend his money.

One day he told Harry 'I've had enough,
'I'm thinking of giving it up.'
Harry tried to persuade him to carry on
but Dave wouldn't listen.
'No,' he said. 'I really don't want to.'
Then Harry said, 'I'll tell you what.
Just do one more trip. A big one.
I'll make sure you earn a fortune on it.
How about it?'

Dave couldn't resist.
He didn't seem to have a will
of his own any more.
'OK,' he said.
'Next weekend – but that's the last one.'

On Friday, Harry came to see him at the office.
'The money's in the briefcase,' he said.
He placed an envelope in front of him.
It contained airline tickets for Hong Kong.

'The Far East?' Dave said.
'But I've not done business there before.'
'No problem,' said Harry.
'You'll be met at the airport.
Hand over the money, like usual.
They'll give you the stuff in a suitcase.
Just get it back safely.'

On Saturday, Dave woke and got ready
to catch the train for Heathrow.
Kylie was lying in bed,
her eyes swollen with crying.
They had had a row the night before.
She didn't want him to go on another trip.
She had had enough of it all.

'I'm off,' he said as he closed his suitcase.

Kylie slowly turned to look at him.
'If you go to Hong Kong,' she said,
'we're finished.
I won't be here when you get back.'
Dave stared at her but he said nothing
and walked out of the door.

7

The Final
Job

Dave sat in the train and thought about Kylie.
She said that he never thought about her,
he only thought about money.
Dave closed his eyes. That was rubbish!
Then he put it out of his mind until he
reached Euston.

He was walking up the ramp when he
suddenly felt ill.
A blinding pain shot through his head.
He staggered a little way forward
and grabbed for a rail.

'Let me help you,' a man said and held him by
the elbow.
'You look awful,' said his wife. 'Maybe you
should go home.'
The couple were kind.
They made him sit down for a while.
And as the pain eased
– he knew that what Kylie said was true.
He had changed.
He was living the life of a crook
and he was going to lose Kylie because of it.
'I have to get back to my wife,' he said.
'She's the best thing that ever happened to me.'

There was a train leaving in three minutes.
If he got that one, Kylie might still be at home.
He hurried for the platform.
He kept going until his lungs were bursting.
Just as the guard raised his flag,
Dave flung open the nearest door and jumped in.
Panting for breath, he flopped
into an empty seat.
He needed a drink. He felt ill.
In fact, he couldn't remember
when he last felt really well.
Yes, he could!
It was the day he stole the briefcase.
That was when things started to happen.

He needed a drink.
Slowly, he looked at the young man opposite.
He was wearing a cheap suit like he used to wear.
'I was happy then,' Dave said to himself
and sighed.
He leaned forward.
'Excuse me,' he said.
'Would you mind looking after my briefcase?
I want to go to the buffet car.'
The young man nodded.
Dave got to his feet and walked down the
rocking train.

'Double whiskey,' he said
when he reached the bar.
He downed it in one. Then he ordered another.
But before he could drink it, he felt a hand
grip his shoulder.
He turned and saw Harry staring at him.

'I thought you'd chicken out on our deal!'
he said.
'So where's the money, whimp?'
Dave felt numb. He couldn't speak
or call for help.
The last sound that he heard
was the train door opening
and the rush of wind as he fell
onto the track below.

The young man stared at Dave's briefcase
on the table in front of him.
It must have cost a bomb.
He reached out and ran his fingers
over the leather.
It was so soft! So smooth!
He wondered if he would ever be able to afford
a briefcase like that.
The young man didn't want to make do with a
plastic briefcase.
No way! He wanted to be RICH!